16 Duets for F Horn or E♭ Horn

Two For Easter

James Curnow

Order Number: CMP 1138-06-401

James Curnow
Two For Easter
F Horn / E♭ Horn

ISBN-10: 90-431-2565-2
ISBN-13: 978-90-431-2565-9

Two For Easter

Sixteen Unaccompanied Duets for Easter
For any instruments

Easter Greetings!

Music at Easter is an extremely important part of celebrating this most wonderful time of year. As we celebrate the resurrection of our Lord, music adds much joy to the celebration.

These easy duets are designed to allow the average to advanced players the opportunity to perform in church, school, or anywhere Easter is being celebrated. No accompaniment is necessary. They may be played by any combination of woodwind, brass, string or mallet percussion instruments.

Below is an instrumentation guide that tells you the appropriate book to purchase for your instrument. For example, an instrument in C may combine with an instrument in Bb, Eb, F, Bass Clef or any Mallet Percussion instrument, or a Bb instrument may combine with instruments in C, Bb, F, Bass Clef or any Mallet Percussion instrument, etc. by purchasing the books in the appropriate key.

Most of all have fun and join in the celebration.

James Curnow
Composer/arranger

Instrumentation Guide

C Instruments (CMP 1135-06-401) Piccolo, Flute, Oboe, Violin, or any Mallet Percussion instrument.

Bb Instruments (CMP 1136-06-401) Clarinet, Bass Clarinet, Comet, Trumpet, Flugel Horn, Tenor Saxophone (play first part only), Trombone T.C., Euphonium/Baritone T.C., Tuba T.C. (play second part only).

Eb Instruments (CMP 1137-06-401) Alto Clarinet, Alto Saxophone, & Baritone Saxophone (play second part only), Tuba T.C. (play second part only).

F/Eb Instruments (CMP 1138-06-401) F/Eb Horn

Bass Clef Instruments (CMP 1139-06-401) Cello, Double Bass (play second part only), Bassoon, Trombone B.C., Euphonium/Baritone B.C., Tuba B.C. (play second part only).

Table of Contents

F HORN

TWO FOR EASTER

Arr. **James Curnow** (ASCAP)

1. CHRIST AROSE

Robert Lowry

2. CROWN HIM WITH MANY CROWNS
(Diademata)

George J. Elvey

3. O SACRED HEAD, NOW WOUNDED

Hans L. Hassler

(Passion Chorale)

4. COME YE FAITHFUL, RAISE THE STRAIN

Arthur S. Sullivan

(St. Kevin)

5. CHRIST THE LORD IS RISEN TODAY

from *Lyrica Davidica*

(Easter Hymn)

6. WERE YOU THERE?

Traditional

7. LO! HE COMES IN CLOUDS DESCENDING

Henry T. Smart

(Sicilian Hymn)

8. REJOICE, THE LORD IS KING
(Darwall)

John Darwall

9. FAIREST LORD JESUS

From *Schleische Volkslieder*

10. REJOICE, YE PURE IN HEART

Arthur H. Messiter

11. ALL HAIL THE POWER OF JESUS NAME
(Coronation)

Oliver Holden

12. THINE IS THE GLORY
(Judas MacCabeus)

George F. Handel

13. JESUS SHALL REIGN
(Duke Street)

John Hatton

14. COME, THOU ALMIGHTY KING

Felice de Giardini

(Italian Hymn)

15. AT THE CROSS

Ralph Hudson

16. COME, CHRISTIANS, JOIN TO SING

Traditional

TWO FOR EASTER

Arr. **James Curnow** (ASCAP)

1. CHRIST AROSE

Robert Lowry

2. CROWN HIM WITH MANY CROWNS
(Diademata)

George J. Elvey

3. O SACRED HEAD, NOW WOUNDED

(Passion Chorale)

Hans L. Hassler

4. COME YE FAITHFUL, RAISE THE STRAIN
(St. Kevin)

Arthur S. Sullivan

5. CHRIST THE LORD IS RISEN TODAY

from *Lyrica Davidica*

(Easter Hymn)

6. WERE YOU THERE?

Traditional

7. LO! HE COMES IN CLOUDS DESCENDING

(Sicilian Hymn)

Henry T. Smart

8. REJOICE, THE LORD IS KING
(Darwall)

John Darwall

9. FAIREST LORD JESUS

From *Schleische Volkslieder*

10. REJOICE, YE PURE IN HEART

Arthur H. Messiter

11. ALL HAIL THE POWER OF JESUS NAME
(Coronation)

Oliver Holden

12. THINE IS THE GLORY
(Judas MacCabeus)

George F. Handel

Majestically (♩ = 112)

13. JESUS SHALL REIGN
(Duke Street)

John Hatton

14. COME, THOU ALMIGHTY KING

(Italian Hymn)

Felice de Giardini

15. AT THE CROSS

Ralph Hudson

16. COME, CHRISTIANS, JOIN TO SING

Traditional